THE BIBLE, THE CHRISTIAN, AND
SPIRITUALISTS

BY

GORDON R. LEWIS

Timothy C. J. Quef
1979

PRESBYTERIAN AND REFORMED PUBLISHING CO.
PHILLIPSBURG, NEW JERSEY
1978

THE AUTHOR

Dr. Gordon R. Lewis, Professor of Theology at Conservative Baptist Theological Seminary in Denver, Colorado, hails from Johnson City, New York. He began his theological education there at Baptist Bible Seminary, earned the A.B. in Theology at Gordon College (1948) and the graduate B.Th. at Faith Theological Seminary (1951). Adding an A.M. in philosophy from Syracuse University (1953), he did work at Cornell University and culminated his philosophical studies with a Ph.D. from Syracuse (1959).

Before coming to the Denver Seminary in 1958, Dr. Lewis pastored the People's Baptist Church, Hamilton Park, Delaware (1949-51), and taught seven years at Baptist Bible Seminary as Professor of Apologetics and Philosophy. While teaching he has held several interim pastorates in New York and Colorado. His wife graduated from Shelton College where she majored in Christian Education. The family includes two girls and a boy.

Published articles by Professor Lewis have appeared in *The Collegiate Challenge, Christianity Today,* and the *Bulletin of the Evangelical Theological Society.* For his Master's thesis, he critically examined Reinhold Niebuhr's influential view of dialectical truth, and for his dissertation Augustine's classical position on faith and reason.

Elected to the Theta Beta Phi Honorary Philosophical Society of Syracuse University, Dr. Lewis is also a member of the American Philosophical Association, The Metaphysical Society of America, The American Academy of Religion, and the Evangelical Theological Society.

PREFACE

Of little value are religious discussions which misrepresent positions, magnify incidentals, or manifest poor spirit. This study attempts to avoid all three pitfalls. A fair hearing is given to the group's primary sources. To eliminate unimportant issues attention has been focused upon the Bible's unique authority and the gospel's central claims. The intention has been to set forth the gospel to others in the same spirit the author would like to meet in those who differ with him.

Beliefs on which a person stakes his spiritual life for time and eternity necessarily concern him deeply. Because these issues are so important, it is hoped that each reader — whatever his emotional involvements — will carefully consider the scriptural conditions of eternal life.

Use of the term "cult" is not intended to disparage any person or association of persons. It is meant to point up a difference not covered by "denomination." Christian denominations, in spite of their intramural debates on other theological and ecclesiastical matters, give preeminence to the gospel of Christ. Cults, on the other hand, while claiming to be Christian alter or minimize the core of Christian faith — the gospel. This study goes forth with the prayer that all who claim to be followers of Christ may personally trust the Savior who was God, became flesh, died for our sins, and rose again, according to the Scriptures.

The author wishes to express his gratitude to the Reverend Edward L. Hayes, Associate Professor of Christian Education at Conservative Baptist Theological Seminary, for preparing the sections entitled "Teaching Suggestions."

The Biblical citations, unless otherwise indicated, are from the *New American Standard Bible* (La Habra, Calif.: Foundation Press, publisher for the Lockman Foundation, 1963).

Part VII

The Bible, The Christian, and Spiritualists

Tearfully we finally leave behind a loved one's fresh grave. In this life we shall not again hear his familiar voice; we shall not again see his familiar form. Not, that is, unless we become Spiritualists!

According to Spiritualism we may see our departed loved one again. His familiar form may materialize before our eyes. Or we may become clairvoyant and see him in the spirit-world. He may communicate with us through coded rappings, or we may hear him speak by clairaudience. At first we may lack sufficient sensitivity to vibrations from the spirits and require the help of a psychically perceptive medium. But the bereaved need not remain in uncertainty or sorrow concerning the departed's continued existence and happiness. Through many different means, Spiritualists insist, the possibility of communication with the dead is very much alive.

Capitalizing upon people's deepest emotions, some swindlers deliberately deceive the sorrowing with stage-managed tricks. Or they use bona fide spiritistic phenomena for unethical purposes. Frauds like these, Palmer Emerson explains, might be called spiritists, but not spiritualists.[1] Their interest is limited to the strange phenomena and "the loaves and fishes" of material profit. Spiritualists, on the other hand, not only know Spiritualism as a science, but accept it as a philosophy and practice it as a religion. Recognizing the reality of the spirit world, the Spiritualist endeavors to mold his or her character and conduct in accordance with its highest teachings. Emphasizing the golden rule, spiritualists may be fine relatives, good neighbors and dependable employees.

Not all interest in Spiritualism is profiteering or religious. While both the insincere and sincere forms probably go back to Old Testament history, recently an attempt has been made to examine spirit-communication from a strictly scientific perspective. Such psychical research includes as well, other forms of extrasensory perception. Parapsychology studies "psychological events which seem to go beyond the normal, recognized, everyday activities of the psyche, providing evidence which seems inexplicable except in terms either of the intervention of some entity other than ourselves or the play of some function other than our known faculties and the senses recognized by contemporary physiology."[2] Although this field is still relatively young, its existence and findings ought not be ignored in religious discussions of Spiritualism.

In one form or another Christians are likely to confront Spiritualism's claims with increasing frequency. Since 1848, when "Old Splitfoot's" raps told the Fox sisters of Hydesville, New York, that his body was buried beneath their house and named his murderer, modern Spiritualism has surged forward. The house rebuilt in Lily Dale, New York, is now a Mecca for thousands of Spiritualists every summer.[3] The *Centennial Book of Modern Spiritualism in America*, issued by The National Spiritualist Association in 1948, described one hundred years of growth in United States Spiritualist Churches.

In 74 years the Brazilian Spiritual Federation claims 3,600 centers and 10 million of Brazil's 61 million population, rating *Time* Magazine's designation as the nation's "fastest growing cult."[4] Normandy may be the beachhead for Spiritualism in France, with hundreds of sorcerers practicing in 300 Spiritualist temples.[5] In all of France, it is estimated, some 75,000 diviners and clairvoyants of all kinds receive annually about 750,000,000 francs (roughly $2,000,000).[6] The English healing medium, Harry Edwards, who frequently receives 2,000 letters a day, compiled statistics showing improvement in 80% of his patients and cures with 30%.[7] Every Sunday night a quarter of a million people in Britain attend meetings to receive messages from the spirits.[6] Attunement with spirit power is becoming big business.

What shall evangelical Christians think of Spiritualism as a religion? Is it a form of Christianity? Are Spiritualist acquaintances forgiven their sins and in fellowship with God? How may a believer in Christ help a Spiritualist? Seven questions may guide discussions to the central message of Christianity and the basis on which it rests.

Authority

In order to help Spiritualists consider the unique importance of Scripture inspired by the Holy Spirit, Christians may ask them, "Do you base your religious teachings on revelations or sacred writings other than the Bible?"

In reply Spiritualists will most likely quote from the National Association's Declaration of Principles: "We affirm that the Precept of Prophecy contained in the Bible is a Divine attribute proven through Mediumship."[9] What does this mean? Spiritualism does not rest on the Bible, but the Bible rests on spiritualistic experiences. B. F. Austin explains, "The Bible so far as it is inspired and true is based upon Mediumship and therefore both Christianity . . . and Spiritualism rest on the same basis. Spiritualism does not depend for its credentials and proofs upon any former revelation."[10] In so far as the Bible displays supernormal knowledge, that is alleged to come from mediums. But the Bible is not in its entirety inspired revelation from God. The real basis of Spiritualism is not the Bible, it is the experience of the individual Spiritualists. For example, Christians believe in life after death as taught in inspired Scripture. But Sir Oliver Lodge said, "I know that certain friends of mine who have died still exist, because I have talked with them!"

Unsatisfied with what stands written, Spiritualists crave secret information. "The underlying thought in all forms of divination is that by employing certain means men are able to obtain knowledge otherwise beyond their reach."[11] God has not deemed it wise to reveal everything. "The secret things belong unto the Lord our God: but those things which are revealed belong unto us and to our children forever, that we may do all the words of this law" (Deut. 29:29). Surely in the Bible we have more than we can fulfill. It is all inspired and profitable that the man of God may be perfect, thoroughly furnished unto all good works" (I Tim. 3:16-17).

What may be said to Spiritualists who remain unwilling to submit to Biblical teaching alone as inspired? For the sake of argument suppose the Spiritualists were right at this point. Suppose people were to obtain guidance now from spirits of the dead. Then to whom shall they go when contact cannot be made? For eighteen years Claude D. Noble tried to contact the spirits of Darrow and Thurston. According to a pact made when they were alive, the survivor would hold an object associated with the deceased on the anniversary of his death and his spirit would knock it out of the survivor's hand. That would break the barrier between life and death. But Noble says, "Nothing has ever happened." And rather than appoint a successor for the fruitless vigil, he adds, "I've been at this for 18 years and nothing has come of it. I think I'll let it die with me."[12] On what shall he base his confidence in life after death? If his life was to be governed by the highest teachings from the spirit world, by what standard has his religious faith and life been governed these 18 silent years?

When communications allegedly do come from the dead, it is a problem to determine whether the message is true or false. Its source could be a "naughty spirit" or *Poltergeist* bent upon deceiving. Such influential Spiritualists as William Crookes and Sir Conan Doyle admitted that there is no known test by which you can tell a bona fide spirit from a deceiver.[13] Furthermore in the afterlife spirits retaining a sense of humor may enjoy practical jokes at our expense! Of one instance, Sir Oliver Lodge said, "Silly spirits wanted to have a game."[14] They may even give bad counsel in fields outside the scope of their knowledge. A University of Michigan professor sued a Detroit medium for $16,000 because at her advice he lost his money in a bad investment. But she claimed in no way to be responsible since she merely put him in contact with Thomas Carlyle, the Scottish essayist and historian.[15]

Spiritualists admit not only that the spirits may deceive, play jokes, and blunder, but that a medium's purported spirit-message may not come from the spirits at all. In accounting for the failure of spirit messages regarding worldly affairs, B. F. Austin alludes to the sitter's very strong desire and will (a frequent circumstance among those consulting mediums) and admits:

> The medium in a sensitive condition is more largely dominated by vibrations of the sitter than by the vibrations of the spirit world and the sitter gets back a reflex of his own mind and will. Sometimes the mortal vibrations of a circle are stronger than those from the spirit realm. A sitter under such conditions gets back the message he has brought.[16]

To take spirit-communiques as the sole source of serious religious commitments, some test must be devised by which to know whether or not they are falsehoods, jokes, or mere self-projections.

But suppose spirit-messages do come and convey truth, how much is really learned? "Take all the spiritualistic messages ever received at their face value," concludes G. W. Butterworth in *Spiritualism and Religion,*

and they add nothing significant to human knowledge, no fresh scientific truth, no development of art, no pregnant saying. If all that survived were a shadow life, capable of retaining a feeble identity for a time, till like a cloud of smoke it vanished into space we should expect very much the same kind of messages that Spiritualism provides us with today.[17]

Is this a sufficient basis for an entire religion? Granted that the real person does survive the burial of his body, what shall we believe about God and the world, man and sin, Christ and salvation, the Holy Spirit and the Christian life, the Christian church and things to come in our troubled world? On some of today's most urgent religious problems Spiritualism's best contributions have nothing to say.

And just how certain is the Spiritualist's case for life after death? Has immortality been scientifically proved? Spiritualists who claim it has want their theories to be received as a science. What then is the verdict of competent psychical research? Henry Sidgwick, founder of the Society for Psychical Research, related his conclusions to William James, who wrote:

Like all founders, Sidgwick hoped for a certain promptitude of results: and I heard him say, the year before his death, that if anyone had told him at the outset that after twenty years he would be in the same identical state of doubt and balance that he started with, he would have deemed the prophecy incredible. It appeared impossible that that amount of handling evidence should bring so little finality of decision.

And what was the considered judgment of the noted American psychologist, William James? He continues:

My own experience has been similar to Sidgwick's. For twenty-five years I have been in touch with the literature of psychical research, and have been acquainted with numerous "researchers." I have also spent a good many hours (though far fewer than I ought to have spent) in witnessing (or trying to witness) phenomena. Yet I am theoretically no "further" than I was at the beginning; and I confess that at times I have been tempted to believe that the Creator has

9

eternally intended this department of nature to remain *baffling*, to prompt our curiosities and hopes and suspicions all in equal measure, so that, although ghosts and clairvoyances, and raps and messages from spirits, are always seeming to exist and can never be fully explained away, they also can never be susceptible of full corroboration.[18]

More recent studies may confirm the occurrence of remarkable phenomena, but not the hypothesis that they are produced by spirits. Mrs. Eileen J. Garrett, for years a highly successful medium, has abandoned the spirit hypothesis in favor of a "magnetic field" into which our natural powers can reach. What are now regarded the supernormal perception of the few, she expects to become the gradually accepted powers of the many.[19] At Duke University J. B. Rhine's carefully controlled experiments, with thousands of instances statistically eliminating possibilities of fraud and chance, have, in the judgment of men like Dr. Shaefer, Professor of Physics at the University of Heidelberg, "established the reality of these phenomena as far as telepathy and clairvoyance are concerned.[20] And this is the conclusion of Reginald Omez, who writes the volume on *Psychical Phenomena* for the *Twentieth Century Encyclopedia of Catholicism*. Philosopher Antony Flew, in *A New Approach to Psychical Research*, joins the psychologist Thouless in maintaining that "evidence for the reality of the phenomena is now so overwhelming that scepticism can only be justified by ignorance of the experimental results."[21] None of these scholars, however, accepts the Spiritualist hypothesis.

Commitment to Spiritualistic phenomena as the authoritative source and test of truth remains scientifically unjustified, philosophically tenuous, and religiously meager. How tragic to confine oneself to such ambiguous phenomena when Jesus Christ came to give life and life abundantly (Jn. 10:10). He came not to destroy the law and the prophets but to fulfill them (Mt. 5:17-18). Christians, having found abundant life through the written Word (Jn. 20:31), will share their Biblically founded assurance so that Spiritualists may know that they have eternal life (I Jn. 5:13).

It is not enough to accept the Bible as the primary source and final test of truth; it must be soundly interpreted. Christian Scientists accept the Bible as interpreted by Mary Baker Eddy's *Science and Health with Key to the Scriptures*. Mormons accept the Bible as interpreted by Joseph Smith's *Book of Mormon, Doctrines and Covenants,* and *Pearl of Great Price.* Similarly Spiritualists claim that "Modern Spiritualism furnishes the KEY to the Bible."[22] In all three cults the alleged Biblical ideas are extremely different. The one Bible cannot teach flat contradictions.

If anyone seriously wants to know what the Bible teaches, he may discover the author's meaning by studying his entire work in terms of his life, culture, language, style, and purpose. To introduce into any piece of literature "key" ideas unknown to the author is to destroy the intended meaning. At this point every writer who expects a fair hearing must practice the golden rule with other writers. If he alters the meaning of a sentence or paragraph, can he ethically claim the original author's support for the idea? According to the Bible itself people may handle it deceitfully (II Cor. 4:2) and twist it to their own destruction (II Pet. 3:16). Christians are concerned that they themselves and their Spiritualist friends avoid that grave danger.

When Spiritualists assert that their views coincide with primitive Christianity they alter the meanings of Bible writers. Admitting this, D. Mona Berry writes, "By a slight change of name, 'medium' for 'prophet,' 'clairvoyant' for 'discernment of spirits,' 'psychic phenomena' for 'miracles,' 'spirit lights' for 'tongues of fire,' the close affinity of the two systems becomes apparent to all sincere investigators and students."[23] Reminiscent of Mary Baker Eddy's glossary of terms, this "slight change of name" makes the Bible endorse what its writers emphatically opposed! The prophets received their messages, not from spirits of the dead, but from God. Spirits were discerned (I Cor. 12:10) not by clairvoyant apprehension, but by their teaching about Jesus Christ (I Jn. 4:1-3). Biblical miracles, unlike Spiritualistic phenomena, took place in nature and in broad daylight. They served not to entertain or comfort a mere individual but to establish God's redemptive program. And Pentecost was hardly "the greatest Seance in history"[24]—not one voice from departed dead was heard. Rather the Holy Spirit came, with attendant indications like fire and wind, as Jesus promised. Never in the New Testament are Christians engrossed in communing with spirits of their dead. After a thorough examination of alleged spiritualism in the Bible, G. W. Butterworth eloquently says,

11

When Stephen was stoned and James the brother of John was beheaded, how many disciples must there not have been whose hearts yearned for a word from these brave young men whom they had known and loved? Yet the record is silent concerning them. The early Church, like an army, pursues its way. It knows that some must fall, and their loss is an occasion for mingled sorrow and pride. But it cannot spare time to linger in the thought of them. . . . No doubt their names were recalled in the services of the local churches in which the martyrs were known. Every Christian would be taught that there was a "communion of saints" and that the veil which separated life from death was a thin one. But it was God who mattered. If living and departed were alike in communion with him, they were not far from each other. There the problem must be confidently left "until the day break, and the shadows flee away."[25]

Nevertheless Joseph P. Whitwell says that the NSAC's Declaration of Principles means "belief and acceptance of the truths which are contained in the Bible."[26] Apparently he refers to the "truths" Spiritualists read into the Bible. As George Lawton found, "Spiritualists argue the existence of a spirit world from mediumistic messages and discover mediumistic powers whenever a description of a spiritual world is found. They spiritualize at will preceding philosophies."[27]

In 1907 the Progressive Spiritual Church withdrew from the National Spiritualist Association of Churches, insisting that its members accept a confession of faith based not upon the N.S.A.'s Declaration of Principles but upon the authority of the Holy Bible.[28] However, authorities, even in written form, become insignificant in comparison with their intensely individual experience. "What need has the believer of the verbal testimony of others who are reporting on events which transpired thousands of years previously, what need has he of written authority when he has the testimony of his own eyes and ears!"[29] Spiritualists put the fallible word of departed human spirits above the infallible Word of God's Holy Spirit. How much better to acknowledge the possibility of misinformation in spirit messages and to accept the Scripture as the only inerrant test of truth. Genuine Christian experience never contradicts plain Bible teaching.

Summing up, if for our religious authority we take spirit messages, the spirits may fail to communicate. If they do communicate, we cannot tell whether the message is a lie, a blunder, a joke, or a reflex of our own minds. Because the content of spirit messages is so limited many of our most urgent questions will go unanswered. Even the "proof" for life after death remains a disputed theory. Spiritualism reads into Scripture ideas not held by its authors and denies, in practice at least, that the Bible teaches God's inspired truth.

The Priority of the Gospel

A second question focuses attention on the Bible's central message. Christians may ask Spiritualists: "Is your main business the preaching of the gospel?" What answer may be anticipated?

There may be uncertainty about the nature of the gospel. If so, have them read I Corinthians 15:3,4, where Paul sets forth the gospel he preached. Christ (the anointed one of God the Father) died for our sins, was buried and the third day rose again according to the Scriptures. Anticipated by God's Old Testament people, enacted by Jesus Christ and proclaimed by all his New Testament followers and the church to this day, the gospel is the core of Christianity. Its declaration should be the Spiritualists' major mission.

However, we search Spiritualist literature in vain for emphasis on the gospel. It is not found in the N.S.A.'s Declaration of Principles.[30] Rather, stress falls upon infinite Intelligence, the golden rule, and endless possibility of self-reformation. No urgent call to decision for Christ in this life determines one's destiny. Neither is the gospel featured in Joseph P. Whitwell's interpretation of the Principles.[31] Rather, he teaches, since all men manifest infinite Intelligence all are children of God. They need no rebirth by the Holy Spirit. By personal striving they make heaven for themselves. Spiritualist writings tell us what man through communication with the departed can do for himself, but not what God has graciously done for man through the incarnation, death, and resurrection of Christ. Like Paul's Jewish brethren, Spiritualists "have a zeal for God, but not according to knowledge. For they being ignorant of God's righteousness, have not submitted themselves unto the righteousness of (which comes from) God" (Rom. 10:2-3). So, like Paul, our

13

"heart's desire and prayer" for Spiritualists is that they might be saved (Rom. 10:1).

What then is the main business of Spiritualism? In the broadest sense Spiritualists would present to the world "the newer and fuller gospel of the Harmonial Philosophy."[32] As such Spiritualism purports to "explain the enigmas and riddles of life. It brings all realms of nature under law and asserts that man's whole duty in life is to find out the laws of nature and conform to them."[33] Unquestionably the major source of this rationalism is spirit-messages. And what is the true mission of spirit-messages? B. F. Austin gives four answers to that question:

> First to convince men of the continuity of human life. Secondly to spiritualize our thoughts, affections and lives by instruction and guidance. Thirdly to bring us Consolation in the sorrows and bereavements of life. Fourthly, to enable us to reach through Mediumship exalted and powerful spiritual helpers in the great crises of life.[34]

The preoccupation with spirit messages is based upon the assumption that after death life continues without the body in the same vicinity. No impassable barrier nor immeasurable distance separates the dead from the living. Only the denseness of the physical body with its interests keeps us from observing the spirit world. Our receptors are not properly attuned to pick up the signals of psychic energy. But just as we know there are sound and light waves above and below our sensory perceptibility, so there are psychic forces. A medium has developed the ability to disengage himself from the usual conscious activities and go into a trance. In that state the medium has varying degrees of sensitivity to communications from the spirit world.

Christians may not differ with the Spiritualist description of the next life, but Christians who govern their lives by Scripture decidedly oppose the Spiritualist's attempt to communicate with the dead. According to Jesus' description in Luke 16, the souls of the unsaved rich man and the saved beggar were both separated by an impassable barrier from the living. The rich man who desperately desired to warn his living brothers of future torment, did not hope for any spirit communication with them. The only possibility of communication seemed to be through a resurected body. Even communication with the resurrected dead, Jesus said, would not make his relatives believe.

Knowing the human heart, our Lord said, "If they hear not Moses and the prophets, neither will they be persuaded though one rose from the dead" (Lk. 16:31). The dead cannot communicate with the living and it would be useless if they could.

How then does the Bible account for spiritualistic phenomena which are not fraudulent or psychologically explained? While people cannot contact spirits of the dead, they can contact evil spirits, or demons. The demons are not spirits of dead people, but fallen angels who, in allegiance with Satan, war against God (Eph. 6:12). A girl who made her masters rich by divination at ancient Philippi was possessed by an unclean spirit (Acts 16:16-18). Their income was cut off, however, when in the name of the Lord Jesus Christ Paul and Silas cast the demon out of her. The ministers of Satan employ superhuman knowledge and power for deceitful purposes (Rev. 9:20-21; 16:13-14). No one committed to Christ and righteousness can offer himself to the sinister purposes of the devil (I Cor. 10:21). Any Spiritualist who desires the highest teaching from the world beyond will avoid any practice which might associate him with the father of lies who was a murderer from the beginning (Jn. 8:44).

Whoever knowingly persists in practices subject to satanic control cuts himself off from God and His blessing. Such apostasy in Israel was punished by death. "The soul that turneth after such as have familiar spirits ('controls'),.and after wizards, to go a whoring after them, I will even set my face against that soul, and will cut him off from among his people. . . he shall surely be put to death; they shall stone him with stones" (Lev. 20:6,27; Ex. 22:18). God's people could not endanger themselves by association with those who joined forces with the wicked one. "Regard not them that have familiar spirits, neither seek after wizards, to be defiled by them: I am the Lord our God" (Lev. 19:31. No man can serve two masters. The potential for evil in spiritualistic phenomena led to such abominations in Canaan that God had to destroy its seven nations. If Israel yielded to the same temptations, she too would be driven out (Dt. 18:9-14). God is no respector of persons. In all righteousness He must judge any who knowingly join the devil's conspiracy. So Manasseh, king of Judah, in spite of his position was put to death (II Kings 21:6). Similarly Israel's first king, Saul, who sought the witch of Endor, lost his throne and his life (I Chron. 10:13-14).

In contrast, whoever would receive the blessings Israel enjoyed must, like Josiah, put away every trace of spiritism. We plead with Spiritualists today as Isaiah did long ago, instead of seeking "wizards that peep and mutter should not a people seek unto their God? . . . To the law and to the testimony: if they speak not according to this word, it is because there is no light in them" (Isa. 8:19-20). "Sorcery" is not highly "spiritual"; it is a product of sinful "flesh" (Gal. 5:20). Having forsaken the Biblically revealed gospel of God's grace, sorcerers remain forever "outside" the holy city, Jerusalem (Rev. 22:15).

According to the Bible, then, Spiritualism's main business is nothing short of devilish business. Spiritualists fail to proclaim the gospel to the ends of the earth. In place of our Lord's great commission they put the consulting of spirits. However comforting the temporary results may be, they cannot usurp the place of redemptive truth. Since Satan disguises himself as an angel of light it is not strange that his servants also disguise themselves as servants of righteousness (II Cor. 11:14-15). The apostle Paul long ago warned that there is no other gospel, only perversions of Christ's gospel. Furthermore, he wrote by the Holy Spirit's inspiration, "if we, or an angel from heaven," should preach to you a message contrary to that gospel, "let him be accursed" (Gal. 1:8-9). One who displaces the gospel with spirit messages cannot escape that plain teaching of God's Word. How urgent, then, is the Spiritualist's need to turn from his perverted gospel to the one true gospel.

Christ

In order to help a Spiritualist find firm faith in God, a Christian directs discussion to Jesus Christ. Jesus said, "I am the way, the truth and the life: no man cometh unto the Father but by me" (Jn. 16:6). And the New Testament further asserts that what we think about Christ is crucial. "Whosoever transgresseth, and abideth not in the doctrine of Christ, hath not God. He that abideth in the doctrine of Christ, he hath both the Father and the Son" (II Jn. 9). A Christian concerned for Spiritualists will ask, "Do you believe that Jesus is the Christ, the eternal Word of the Father who became flesh?" (Jn. 1:1,14). Of the eternal Christ manifest in human form John wrote, "as many as received him, to them gave he power to become the sons of God, even to them that believe on his name" (1:12).

What will a Spiritualist be likely to say about Jesus Christ? A clear expression of the Spiritualist belief appears in B. F. Austin's answers to three specific questions.

> Do Spiritualists deny the existence of the historic Jesus? No. The vast body of Spiritualists, including all their representative writers, accept Jesus as an historical character. They do not deny his miracles, though they hold it is impossible to make certain to human minds the happenings of two thousand years ago. Spiritualists as a body venerate the name and character of Jesus and regard him as the world's great Teacher and Exemplar.
>
> Do Spiritualists believe in the divinity of Jesus? Most assuredly. They believe in the divinity of all men. Every man is divine in that he is a child of God, and inherits a spiritual (divine) nature. Just as a man develops his intellectual and spiritual nature and expresses it in life, he is "God manifest in the flesh." Since Jesus attained to and manifested in a very unusual degree the divine attributes of spirit no spiritualist would question his divinity.
>
> Does Spiritualism recognize Jesus as one person of the Trinity, co-equal with the Father, and divine in a sense in which divinity is unattainable by other men? No. Spiritualism accepts him as one of many Savior Christs, who at different times have come into the world to lighten its darkness and show by precept and example the way of life to men. It recognizes him as a world Savior but not as "the only name" given under heaven by which men can be saved.[35]

Spiritualists should be fully aware that they deny the plain teaching of Scripture: "Neither is there salvation in any other: for there is none other name under heaven given among men, whereby we must be saved" (Acts 4:12). Jesus is not the only Savior, according to Spiritualists, because He is not uniquely the son of God. Jesus differs from other men only in degree, but not in kind, they say. And they may even put this teaching into the mouth of Christ. For example, in a mimeographed letter to clergymen Samuel Jacoby claims to have heard by clairaudience Jesus saying to him:

> I, Jesus of Nazareth, now offer these living declarations as a solution to the world's manifold difficulties - which the clergy are self-mandated to eradicate - will you so help.

17

Give to the people the truth that will make them free - to relieve them of the suspense in which you now hold them - burdening them with a soul bondage of a false concept of me - Jesus of Nazareth - as the God of all creation and created things.

I am not the King of Kings nor the Lord of Lords, as has been put upon me by some of your primitive minded men of the old theological school . . . . we were simple Jewish folks - living an honorable life when gossips began to talk that I was the Messiah . . . Why call me the Lord Jesus Christ, I am not the Lord of Creation, or your God as many of you believe to this day - dismiss these foolish things from your minds - erase them from your books of record.

All of you, my brothers, have the Christ Spirit to find within the latent powers of the Godhead of which you are endowed as I was an am today.

We are called the holy family, but we are no more holy than thou, my brother, nor any of our brethren, only in so much that we are humble servants one to another.[36]

In his own handwriting Samuel Jacoby added:

These trancendent declarations ware prepared by the Father's anointed Son Jesus of Nazareth: the Master Teacher: Who now comes to the world's clergy to remove the abominations of the virus of your theological garbage substituted for the golden rule emphasized by the Master Teacher during his great mission to remove the darkness in the people's mind - for ages - and still today on this entire planet - Why?

The style attributed to Jesus seems remarkably similar to the style of Samuel Jacoby! And the ideas of Jacoby also are quite obviously ascribed to none other than Jesus Christ.

If a message from the spirit world supports the orthodox doctrine of Christ's deity, as one from a Julia did, Spiritualists have a ready escape from the contradiction. They say that a spirit at first tends to think in terms of his old faith. In time a spirit like Julia will realize that Christ is no more a divinity than any other man, but is a great person and teacher.[37] The whole structure of dependence on continued spirit messages falls if "God has in these last days spoken unto us in his Son" (Heb. 1:1) and if the inspired Scripture is sufficient to make the man of God thoroughly furnished to every good work (II Tim. 3:16-17). So Spiritualists will never be able to give Christ or the Bible the preeminent place they hold in Christianity. Spiritualism is not "clarified Christianity" as Rev. Ford asserted; it is blasphemously anti-Christian.[38]

The doctrinal test by which to discern the spirits requires an unqualified confession that Jesus of Nazareth, the Christ (Messiah) is of God (in a way other men are not) (I Jn. 4:1-3). One who does not believe that Jesus Christ has come in the flesh is "a deceiver and an anti-christ" (II Jn. 7). Spiritualists should understand the seriousness of their denial of Christ's deity.

In claiming to be the Son of God, Jesus made it clear to the Jews that He was claiming more than to be a member of the human race (a son of God as all men are by creation). The Jews sought to kill Him because He said that "God was his Father, making himself equal with God" (Jn. 5:18). Upon another occasion Jesus said, "Before Abraham was, I am." And the Jews again tried to stone him for blasphemy. They did the same when he said, "I and my Father are one" (Jn. 10:30). If Jesus taught of Himself what Spiritualists teach, His life would never have been threatened. That He claimed to be far more than a teacher or medium is clear when the Jews told Pilate, "We have a law, and by our law he ought to die, because he made himself the Son of God" (Jn. 19:7). To hold as Spiritualists do that Jesus was not essentially one with the Father is to say that Jesus was a liar or a lunatic. He could not have been, like the founders of other world religions, a great interpreter of truth to his age, if the astounding claims He made for Himself were untrue. So great were these claims that one can only conclude He was Himself a deceiver or seriously deluded. Distinguishing Himself from all others, Jesus said, "Ye are from beneath; I am from above: ye are of this world; I am not of this world" (Jn. 8:23). And Jesus Himself explained the consequences of denying this fact: "if ye believe not that I am he, ye shall die in your sins" (Jn. 8:24).

On the other hand, Jesus promised, "He who believes in Me, as the Scripture said, 'From his innermost being shall flow rivers of living water.' But this He spoke of the Spirit, whom those who believed in Him were to receive; for the Spirit was not yet given, because Jesus was not yet glorified (Jn. 38-39). The higher, richer life which Spiritualists properly seek may be found, not in attempted conversation with human spirits, but by faith in Jesus Christ and the consequent reception of the Holy Spirit. Jesus came that we might have life, and that we might have it abundantly (Jn. 10:10). His promise that believers could do even greater works than He had done (Jn. 14:12) was to be fufilled through prayer in Christ's name and through the help of the Holy Spirit who would remain with them forever (Jn. 14:13-16). Very much aware of the sorrow accompanying a loved one's loss, Jesus promised, "I will not leave you as orphans; I will come to you . . . the Helper, the Holy Spirit, whom the Father will send in My name, He will teach you all things, and bring to your remembrance all that I said to you. Peace I leave with you; My peace I give to you; not as the world gives, do I give to you. Let not your heart be troubled, nor let it be fearful" (Jn. 14:18-27).

Faith in Jesus Christ as the eternal Son of God is not for genuine Christians simply a piece of dead dogmatism. By faith in Christ a person begins a life of communion with God's Spirit. The Holy Spirit assures believers of eternal life and leads throughout this life. "For all who are being led by the Spirit of God, these are the sons of God. . . . The Spirit Himself bears witness with our spirit that we are children of God, and if children, heirs also, heirs of God and fellow heirs with Christ" (Rom. 8:14-17). Through faith in Christ and fellowship with the Holy Spirit Christians receive all the values Spiritualists hope to find in psychic phenomena: certainty of life after death, more spiritual thought, consolation and help in the crises of life. But these are not conditioned upon the uncertainties of seances. They are based upon God's unfailing promises (objectively) and upon the inner communion of the Holy Spirit (subjectively).

Spiritualists might ask the Holy Spirit's illumination as they study other evidence in Scripture for Christ's deity. At His birth Jesus was called Immanuel which means God with us (Mt. 1:23). His miracles were not limited to healings; He raised the dead and controlled the forces of nature. When by a word He calmed the perilous storm, men marveled saying, "What kind of a man is this, that even the winds and the sea obey him" (Mt. 8:27)? Unschooled as He was, His teaching is unexcelled. Although at any time he could have called legions of angels or disappeared, Jesus willingly endured the cross for the sake of others. He died. Three days later he came forth from the grave demonstrating to the world that he had conquered sin and death. Thomas, unbelieving in spite of others' reports, finally saw the evidence for himself and exclaimed, "My Lord and my God" (Jn. 20:28)!

Indeed the eternal Word of God (Jn. 1:1) had become flesh and dwelt among us (Jn. 1:14,18). He who existed in the form of God did not regard equality with God a thing to be grasped, but emptied Himself, taking the form of a bondservant, being made in the likeness of men (Phil. 2:6-7). Jesus Christ was the very radiance of God's glory and the exact representation of God's nature (Heb. 1:3). Higher than any angel, Christ's throne (power) is eternal (Heb. 1:8) and immutable (Heb. 1:10-12). The creator of everything that had a beginning (Jn. 1:3) whether in heaven or earth, visible or invisible (Col. 1:16), Jesus Christ sustains everything in existence to this day (Col. 1:17). Furthermore He heads the Church which He purchased with His own blood (Col. 1:18; Acts 20:28). At present His authority in heaven and earth provides the resource for discipling the world (Mt. 28:18-20). He is building His church and the gates of hell cannot prevail against it (Mt. 16:18). But the time will come when He shall again be revealed from heaven, but this time in flaming fire taking vengeance on those who do not know God and obey the gospel (II Thess. 17:-10). As King of Kings and Lord of Lords He shall finally destroy the powers of evil and establish righteousness forever more (Rev. 19:11 - 22:21).

To believe in Christ simply as a great man, different only in degree from other men, is an affront indeed. "For in him all the fulness of deity dwells in bodily form" (Col. 2:9).

Redemption

As it is all-important to believe that Jesus Christ was God manifest in the flesh, it is equally essential to believe that He died for the sins of the world. Christians concerned about the welfare of Spiritualists will ask them, "Do you believe that Christ's shed blood is the only basis for the forgiveness of your sins?"

A Spiritualist's answer may very well begin by attacking the notion of sin. All men are said to be children of God; a spark of divinity dwells in all.[39] Unthinkable then is the idea that men are born with a sinful nature. Furthermore evolutionary science is thought to have disproved the Biblical teaching on man's sin. Writing in *The National Spiritualist*, Frank D. Warren says,

> The orthodox belief is that the human race began with Adam and Eve. But man did not descend from Adam and Eve but ascended through the natural evolutionary process from lower orders of animal life; and the Infinite Intelligence of Nature has decreed that man shall continue to ascend - the world without end.
>
> Science has proven the Garden of Eden story to be a myth; and orthodox religion is, therefore based upon a myth. The faulty logic is simply staggering. How can a mere belief in atonement through the blood of Jesus save man from the "original sin" of Adam and Eve in the Garden of Eden - when there was no Garden of Eden, and no Adam and Eve, and no "original sin?"[40]

Again Spiritualists must choose their ultimate authority. If they follow the general teaching of their movement, they must deny the Bible's plain teaching. However, Christians, like their Lord, acknowledge that God created Adam and Eve at the beginning (Mt. 19:4). Man is the product not of a gradual moral evolution, but of a righteous Creator. Nevertheless, as Genesis 3 teaches, man sinned. "Therefore just as through one man sin entered into the world and death through sin, so death spread to all men, because all sinned" (Rom. 5:12).

While the Bible insists that God created man in His image, it never minimizes the pervasiveness of fallen man's sin. By nature a child of wrath (Eph. 2:3) man is dead in his trespasses and sins (Eph. 2:1). His mind is blinded to spiritual truth (Eph. 4:18), his desires are evil (Eph. 2:3) and his will is enslaved to sin (Rom. 6: 16-17). Try as he will, he cannot liberate himself (Rom. 7:14-25). Although his conduct frequently appears good to human observation, the best of men comes short of God's perfect standard. Has anyone always kept the golden rule? "There is none righteous, not even one" (Rom. 3:10-23). Man's moral disease is incurable, apart from the atonement of Jesus Christ.

Because Spiritualists fail to admit the pervasiveness of sin they think man is capable of improving himself without any atoning provision of divine love. Asked if Spiritualists recognize any special value or efficacy in the death of Christ for man's salvation, B. F. Austin frankly answered,

No. Spiritualism sees in the death of Jesus an illustration of the martyr spirit, of that unselfish and heroic devotion to humanity which ever characterized the life of Jesus, but no special atoning value in his sufferings and death. The world has had uncounted illustrations of men who have died for the truth. All such deaths have a moral value and influence, but not in a sense of a ransom price for the souls of others, as taught by the so-called orthodox churches.[41]

Spiritualists deny not only that Jesus' death was a ransom, but also that it had any substitutionary value as a penalty for others' sins. In 1908, on the sixtieth anniversary of modern Spiritualism, Professor Hiram Corson of Cornell University said,

The literature of Spiritualism . . . is destined to transform, if not, perhaps in time, do away with, theology . . . and to make THE LIFE OF THE SPIRIT the all in all in religion, as it was the all in all with the founder of Christianity. Jesus taught Salvation comes from WITHIN, not from without. There could be no such thing, in the nature of things, as a vicarious atonement for the sins of the world. Man can be AT ONE with the Universal Spirit only through his own spiritual vitality. That alone is Salvation.[42]

The correspondence from Samuel Jacoby makes Jesus to mouth the typical Spiritualist position. "I have also declared to this instrument to say unto you for me, Jesus of Nazareth - that no man is saved by my blood - just because I was nailed to a cross."[43] Jesus goes on to say, according to Jacoby, that he cannot understand why the same honor was not bestowed on Socrates, who drank the hemlock so nobly.

To the Spiritualist, as to many others, the death of a substitute and the justification of a sinner seems unjust. As Converse E. Nickerson put it, "Man must make his own heaven if he will merit such a celestial happiness; were God to deal otherwise with His offspring it would not be justice to either man or God."[44] If Christians are to help Spiritualists accept the gospel they must, like the apostle Paul, explain how God can at the same time be just and the justifier of one who has faith in Jesus (Rom. 3:26). Christians must be ready to answer Arthur Conan Doyle who wrote, "One can see no justice in a vicarious sacrifice, nor in the God who could be placated by such means. Above all, many cannot understand such expressions as the 'redemption from sin,' 'cleansed by the blood of the lamb,' and so forth."[45]

Several issues are involved in the Christian doctrine of redemption. In the first place people rightly emphasize God's absolute justice. Because of divine justice man's sin must receive its deserved penalty. What a man sows he will reap. But he has sowed the seeds of his own death! " The wages of sin is death" (Rom. 6:23). "The soul that sinneth, it shall die" (Ezek. 18:20). The death of which the Bible writers speak is not only the separation of the spirit from the body (James 2:26), but also the separation of the spirit from God. In the latter sense, often called spiritual death, people are "separate from Christ, excluded from the commonwealth of Israel, and strangers to the covenants of promise, having no hope and without God in the world" (Eph. 2:12). They are at enmity with God, far off from God and strangers to God. Although they owe their very life and breath to God, morally and spiritually they are not children of God, but children of the devil (Jn. 6:44). Apart from the intervention of Christ on their behalf they shall remain separated from God, or spiritually dead, forever.

God would be perfectly just if He allowed all men to reap exactly what they have sowed in eternal death. But God, against whom man has rebelled, is no impersonal principle or law, but a loving being full of mercy and grace. Although we justly deserved His wrath, He showers upon us His goodness. He satisfies His justice and provides for pardon in the death of Jesus Christ. It is not that He sends some third party unrelated to the case. Rather Jesus, who as we saw was one with the Father, willingly took the place of the guilty sinner. The offended Judge pronounces the full penalty in satisfaction of perfect justice. He then steps down from the tribunal, puts his arm around the shoulder of the condemned, and pays his complete penalty. At Calvary He suffered not only an excruciating physical death, but an indescribable separation from the Father — spiritual death. Although without sin Himself, He bore the awful consequences of others' sins (II Cor. 5:21).

United to Christ by faith, sinners meet the full demand of divine justice. And it cannot be exacted a second time. By faith a sinner forms a partnership with Christ. Then before the bar of divine justice the sinner no longer stands alone and condemned. Christ and the believer stand together as one. "In Christ" the believer is declared perfectly righteous and receives the gift of eternal life. Believing in Christ he becomes morally and spiritually a child of God (Jn. 1:12).

As a member of the divine family he is a joint-heir with Jesus Christ of all the riches of divine glory (Rom. 8:17). Legally adopted into God's family, the believer's sonship depends, not upon what he does, but upon what Christ did. The Christian lives for God, not out of fear, but out of gratitude. Lovingly he does his best to honor the One who ransomed him from the slave market of sin.

The death of Jesus Christ, then, is far more than an example of selfless devotion. It is at the same time the satisfaction of divine justice and gift of divine grace. By the offering of Christ God remains just and justifies those who believe in Christ (Rom. 3:24-26). No longer spiritually dead while they live, believers enjoy spiritual life. Through the blood of Christ's cross they are reconciled to God and at peace with Him. In loving acceptance and joyful communion they fellowship with God for time and eternity. Far from denying the efficacy of His death, as Jacoby alleged, Jesus regarded it the major purpose for His incarnate life. What Christ really said was, "the Son of Man did not come to be served, but to serve, and to give His life a ransom for many" (Mk. 10:45).

Some very religious Jews in New Testament times thought they could earn their own way to heaven without Christ's atonement for their sin. The urgent warning of the book of Hebrews to them still applies to Spiritualists:

> Anyone who has set aside the Law of Moses dies without mercy on the testimony of two or three witnesses. How much severer the punishment do you think he will deserve who has trampled under foot the Son of God, and has regarded as unclean the blood of the covenant by which he was sanctified, and has insulted the Spirit of grace? For we know Him who said, "Vengeance is mine, I will repay." And again, "The Lord will judge His people." It is a terrifying thing to fall into the hands of a living God. (Heb. 10:28-31).

How much better to be able to say with Paul, "having been justified by his blood, we shall be saved from the wrath of God through him" (Rom. 5:9). All who will may enjoy the reassurance of the Scripture which says, "Therefore having been justified by faith, we have peace with God through our Lord Jesus Christ" (Rom. 5:1). The Christian's prayer to God for Spiritualists is that they might know that peace!

Christ's Resurrection

Another integral part of the gospel the Christian shares with his fellow-men affirms that, having died for our sins, the third day Jesus rose from the grave. The Bible says, "if you confess with your mouth Jesus as Lord, and believe in your heart that God raised him from the dead, you shall be saved" (Rom. 10:9). Because the Scriptures make belief in Christ's resurrection a condition of salvation, Christians ask Spiritualists: "Do you believe that Jesus rose from the dead?"

In answering this question Spiritualists may employ terms with meanings quite strange to the Christian context of thought. If they affirm belief in Christ's resurrection, they probably mean that His spirit materialized before sitters at seances. Interpreted as some sort of confirmation of spiritualistic phenomena, they may accept the idea. As such it would be an event repeatable according to laws of the spirit world. But if Christ's resurrection was a once-for-all physical miracle accomplished in the world of ordinary observation by the free and gracious purpose of almighty God, difference will become apparent.

Spiritualists suggest that the appearances of Christ after His death were materializations, the disappearance of His body, apportism, and the lifting of the stone, levitation. All of this, according to the Easter service in the Spiritualist Manual, was "governed by Natural Law." And it is inferred that psychic phenomena today are produced by the same law. So we may be able to do even greater things.[46] Like all spiritualist phenomena, the resurrection of Christ was intended to prove simply that personal identity continues after death.

> What would be the purpose of this demonstration if it had no bearing upon the lives of all of us? Only something mysterious, and undefinable to believe in? The phenomena of nature is [sic!] a mystery until we understand it, but only in unbiased earnest seeking for an explanation shall we find the answer. . . . It is incumbent upon all of us to tarry in the city of Jerusalem. In other words, the seat of knowledge - our churches, classrooms and seances to become endued with power from on high, since all power resides in knowledge and understanding, when the stone of the sepulchre will be rolled away only to find that our departed loved ones are right in our midst - living entities eager to reveal themselves to us.[47]

And Spiritualists like to say that their evidence for life after death is "a million fold stronger than the evidence the world possesses of the truth of historical Christianity" (that is, for the resurrection).[48] Christians, then, must be prepared to discuss the nature of Christ's resurrection, its significance, and the evidence in support of it.

Was the resurrection of Christ an instance of materialization or a unique miracle in the redemptive plan of God? In materialization a spirit allegedly assumes or causes other things to assume a visible form. Ectoplasm (a "supernormal protoplasmic substance") emanates from the body of the medium and produces physical effects. Alleged photographs of such materializations show fogginess around the edges of an "umbilical cord" to the mouth of the medium.[49] An apport is the alleged supernormal movement of an object, and levitation refers to the raising of objects from the ground by supposed supernormal means. All of this is thought to happen in accord with regular psychic laws.

The Spiritualist's hypothesis, ingenious as it may be, fails to account for the varied data of Christ's resurrection. To begin with, the resurrection appearances of Christ were totally unexpected and spontaneous. They were not sought for nor contrived by any preparations in a seance room. Butterworth, after patient analysis, concludes, "There is no genuine parallel between these stories of various and spontaneous appearances, indoors and out of doors, and the carefully prepared phenomena, held in darkened rooms, of modern Spiritualism."[50] The appearances occurred to men and women, to individuals alone and to groups of up to eleven, and on one occasion five hundred at once. Sometimes Jesus talked with them, sometimes He walked with them for miles, sometimes He started a fire, cooked fish and ate with them. His appearance was not foggy in the least. Some at first thought he was a gardener or an ordinary stranger walking along the same road. No medium was required and He was not limited by any ectoplasmic "umbilical cord." As abruptly as the appearances began they ceased. No ghostlike apparition could have transformed the despairing disciples into courageously sincere witnesses to the risen Christ. When the frightened disciples in a locked room at first thought they had seen a spirit, Jesus Himself said, "Why are you troubled, and why do doubts arise in your hearts? See my hands and my feet, that it is I myself; touch me and see, for a spirit does not have flesh and bones as you see that I have"

(Lk. 24:38-39). He then asked if they had anything to eat. They handed Him a piece of broiled fish and He ate it in their sight.

The evidence for Christ's physical resurrection is abundant and varied. That a Spiritualist should claim there are but two eye-witnesses to the resurrection shows utter disregard for evidence. B. F. Austin ignores some 498 others in order to make the exaggerated claim that evidence for Spiritualism is "a million fold stronger!" A quick reading of I Corinthians 15:1-9 apart from the concluding chapters of each Gospel is sufficient to display the irresponsibility of such allegations. But it is not merely a question of the amount of evidence, it is also a matter of the quality of evidence. The Biblical records have for the last two hundred years been subject to the most severe types of literary and historical criticism. Because the various hypotheses based on laws of nature failed to account for aspects of the data, recent scholars have tended to abandon the attempt to give rationalistic explanations of the narrative as it stands.[51] Spiritualists might well follow the experts in this regard.

Furthermore, from the Biblical point of view, the purpose of the resurrection includes far more than certification of a spirit-life after death. Among other things, Christ's resurrection proves to all men that He is the Son of God (Rom. 1:4), and the world's appointed (Acts 17:30-31). It certifies that everyone who believes on Him has received the forgiveness of sins (Acts 10:43) and justification (Rom. 4:25). The risen Christ is exalted above every other creature to head the church and righteously rule the universe (Eph. 1:20-22). Not only the future resurrection of all men, but their entire salvation from sin is secured by Christ's return to life.

Christians should alert Spiritualists to the tragedy of rejecting the risen Christ: "If Christ has not been raised then your faith is vain, and you are still in your sins" (I Cor. 15:14,17). But Christ has been raised! May Spiritualists trust the One who actually can deliver them from sin as well as the grave!

Personal Trust

The gospel calls for belief in the doctrines of Christ's deity, death, and resurrection, and it calls for more. It challenges all men personally to trust the living Lord. Christians are concerned, then,

GIFT BOOK SEARCHING

Call # or LC #: _BF 1275 . B5_

If owned:

# of copies: Circ. _____ Ref. _____ Study _____

"Walther Library Missing?": _____

Status/Date Due: _____

Issued Count: _____ Soft Issued Count: _____

Last Issued: _____

If not owned:

OCLC #: _34280166_

WorldCat Holdings: _6_

Indiana Holdings: _0_

PALNI Holdings: _0_

☐ Indiana U. ☐ Purdue ☐ Notre Dame ☐ Allen Co.

Notes on Reverse

that Spiritualists also experience this vital relationship. Why not frankly ask, "Are you personally trusting Jesus Christ as your Savior and Lord?"

When referring to faith Spiritualists often deplore a blind or superstitious belief. They also tend to minimize the importance of faith in the sense of religious beliefs. The faith in which they are concerned is the faith that "moves mountains." That kind of faith "is the positive assurance of power, energy and omniscience of God's Eternal Spirit, operating through man in our mundane sphere."[52] Although the faith that moves mountains is said to have "small, if any relation to religious beliefs,"[53] it seems to be joined to one — the belief in life after death. No philosophy is complete without a demonstration of unending life.[54] In this regard reason is called the glorious diadem which God provided to distinguish man from the beasts."[55] Furthermore, "without some certain knowledge of God, how can we worship Him?"[56] This certain knowledge seems largely limited to man's personal mortality. But somehow as a result of this one "demonstrated" fact "Spiritualism puts a new and much broader interpretation on many dogmas taught by the leading religious systems."[57] It is sometimes difficult to see how this "more rational" understanding necessarily follows from Spiritualistic phenomena. Why, for example, is God conceived of in an impersonal pantheistic way?

Christians may point out that they too deplore blind faith or superstitious gullibility. It therefore becomes evident that mountain-moving faith has a closer connection to soundly established religious beliefs than Spiritualists want to admit. From the Christian standpoint it seems narrow-minded indeed to accept evidence of a psychic sort only. Would not a more rational approach openmindedly consider evidence from any source whatsoever? Indications of God's existence and concern for man in time and eternity may be seen in experiences of conversion, answered prayer, communion with God, and fellowship with others in Christ. From the realm of history come "signs" like the origin, dispersion, preservation, and reestablishment of the Jewish people. There is the prophetic preparation for Christ's coming and its marvelous fulfillment. Christ's miracles, in nature as well as human life, culminate in His bodily resurrection and attest His deity. The origin of the Christian church, and the change in the day of worship require an explanation. Add the striking phenomena connected with the Bible and the data converge to support belief in the triune God of the Bible and His redemptive plan stretching through time into eternity. Spiritualists are urged to make as thorough a study of Christian evidences and apologetics as they wish others to make of psychic phenomena.

When a Spiritualist is invited to become a Christian he is not asked to abandon intelligent thought in favor of unfounded faith. The relationship of faith to evidence in Christianity is not totally different from their relationships in other fields. In explaining the given data relevant to a problem, several hypotheses may be considered. The rational man accepts the hypothesis which consistently explains the greatest amount of evidence with the fewest difficulties. But in accepting as true a certain explanation, he exercises faith. Another scientist or physician may diagnose the case differently and exercise his prerogative of choosing another explanation. He may have a different faith. The data remains the same; the interpretations differ. So with psychic phenomena. No one denies what men have actually experienced; but some explanations of the phenomena differ from others. And so it is with Christianity. The experiences of Christians for centuries are given; many believe they can be consistently accounted for only on the assumption that the God of the Bible lives and acts in the way the Scriptures teach He does. Many Spiritualists may not have given this hypothesis a fair hearing. They may never have thoroughly studied the Bible for themselves to see whether the facts may support this conclusion. As people who pride themselves on openness to truth and scientific reasoning, they will want to make this examination. They know too well the irrationality of those who dismiss out of hand their own position. Christianity does not stifle investigation; it welcomes it.

While the evidence for faith may be examined, the object of faith remains unseen. Christians believe in the invisible God and trust His redemptive love. No man has seen God at any time, but "the only begotten" of the Father has made Him known to man (Jn. 1:18). Now Jesus no longer walks the earth. The visible linguistic signs of the Bible now disclose the object of Christian faith. Through taking God at His inspired Word, Christians have found fellowship with Christ. And He has sent the Holy Spirit to dwell in their bodies as in a holy temple. Spiritualists who desire a person to person, rather than a person to creed, relationship, may find it in genuine Christian experience. The experience of faith is not simply a belief in the after life; it is continuous fellowship with the eternal Father, the risen Christ, and the Holy Spirit.

Christian faith is urgent indeed. The decisions of this life settle our eternal destiny. Nowhere in the teaching of Christ or the Bible is there any hope of endless reformation. Any responsible person who passes from this life in unbelief has not the slightest hint of hope. "It is appointed unto man once to die, and after that the judgment" (Heb. 9:27). Since a Spiritualist's eternal destiny is settled in this short life, Christians urge him to believe, and to believe now.

Grace Alone

No permanent happiness or peace may be enjoyed unless a person is right with God. Our relationship to God is ultimately our greatest concern. The question is not how we appear to ourselves, or how we compare with others. Sooner or later we shall face the question of how we appear in God's sight. We dare not simply assume that if we try to be good and do our best that this will meet divine standards. To guide us in our relationship to Him God has given us His Word. In the Bible we learn that God is satisfied with nothing short of perfect righteousness — absolute Christlikeness. By this norm every man has fallen short. All stand condemned by strict justice.

However, apart from anything they deserve, God has arranged to give Christ's perfect righteousness. Those who receive this gift enjoy a proper relationship to Him. They are considered by the Father as righteous as His only begotten Son. Christians stress what the Scripture underlines: "a man is justified by faith apart from works of the law" (Rom. 3:28). That is why Christians ask Spiritualists, "Do you depend upon some acts of your own for your salvation, or is your trust in the grace of God alone?"

Concertedly Spiritualists say, we earn our own way. "We affirm the moral responsibility of the individual that he makes his own happiness or unhappiness as he obeys or disobeys Nature's physical and spiritual laws."[58] The interpretation of this seventh article in the National Spiritualist Association's Declaration of Principles follows:

31

Man himself is responsible for the welfare of the world in which he lives; for its welfare or its misery, for its happiness or unhappiness and if he is to obtain Heaven upon Earth, he must learn to make that heaven, for himself and for others. Individually, man is responsible for his own spiritual growth and welfare. Sins and wrong-doing must be outgrown and overcome. Virtue and love of good must take their place. Spiritual growth and advancement must be attained by aspiration and personal striving. Vicarious atonement has no place in the philosophy of Spiritualism. Each one must carry his own cross to Calvary's Heights in the overcoming of wrong-doing and replacing them with the right.[59]

Spiritualists fail to mention what concerns Christians the most — a person's standing before God. And they plainly disavow any dependence whatsoever upon anything God has done for sinful man.

A number of assumptions are involved. First, Spiritualists teach that man has limitless possibilities. A child is viewed as "a repository of infinite possibilities and not born in sin."[60] All the child needs is training and an avenue of expression. Nature, figuratively speaking, says, "Go out into the world. Make something out of yourself!"[61]

In the second place, Spiritualists assume that knowledge can produce character. "As man thinks God-like thoughts and comes into deific conjunction, he also gains an increasing command of spiritual powers and prerogatives."[62] E. W. Sprague goes so far as to say, "Right thinking is man's true savior." He explains,

It very soon establishes his self-reliance, and self-reliance, coupled with right thinking will develop man's moral nature to the highest point and prepare him to enter into spiritual unfoldment of those higher gifts and faculties that place him in communion with spirits in the spiritual realms.[63]

According to the third assumption, progress is "absolutely certain."[64] God's gracious help is not needed. Even the most degraded personalities in time attain to the greatest heights.[65] It is pointed out, however, that it is easier to begin progression in the earth life. But in various spheres or levels progress persists without end.

Each of these assumptions fails to fit the facts of Scripture and human experience. A child is born in sin (Ps. 51:5). His potentialities are great indeed, but not infinitely great. His sinful nature taints the best of his achievements. Unworthy motives are mixed with wholesome ones. Even prayer, fasting, and almsgiving may be totally unacceptable to God. Like the Pharisees of old, he may adorn the tombs of the prophets, but in God's sight be corrupt (Mt. 23:14-15,23,29). The finest training produces only an educated sinner. Potentially man's discoveries of nuclear power may be used for destructive as well as peaceful purposes. Human possibility is severely curtailed by human depravity.

For the same reason knowledge does not automatically produce character. We all know better than we do. Man is more than a reasoning machine. His appetites and drives often cause him to act in a way quite irrational. And this is as true with the educated as the uneducated. Our finest cultures produce educated criminals. Some are incorrigibly evil. The Bible realistically acknowledges that they remain so eternally. When Jesus said, "You shall know the truth and the truth shall make you free" (Jn. 8:32), He immediately explained, "If therefore the Son shall make you free, you shall be free indeed" (Jn. 8:36). Truth about this world or the world to come does not regenerate. Man's character is basically changed by faith in the sinless Christ who said, "I am the way, the truth and the life" (Jn. 14:6).

And nowhere in Scripture is support found for the notion of absolutely certain progress. The certainty, apart from divine grace, is defection from God's will. Lucifer, the highest of created beings, thinking he would be like the most High became Satan. Adam and Eve with the finest of surroundings chose to gain knowledge of evil as well as good. Cain slew Abel. Wickedness engulfed the world of Noah, the cities of Sodom and Gomorrah, the land of Canaan, and Israel itself in spite of all God's prophets could do. Christ found the people of his day to be in dire need. The disciples were far from perfect and the early church was plagued with problems. The Spiritualists' attempts to build their own heaven, like those of the tower builders at Babel, end in confusion. What is certain is not progress but despair.

Faith, the antidote to despair, simply accepts God's gracious gift of righteousness. The gift from above, of course, is free. No payments remain; Christ paid it all. Human works are not the price of righteousness with God, but the product of righteousness with God. The ransomed lovingly live for their liberator. So the faith that justified is "faith that works by love" (Gal. 5:6). In the Christian's life good works are the fruit of the Holy Spirit.

The Spiritualist's effort to fulfill moral law fails, because of a deficiency not in the golden rule, but in sinful human nature, the "flesh." The Bible explains, "What the Law could not do weak as it was through the flesh, God did: sending his own Son in the likeness of sinful flesh and as an offering for sin, he condemned sin in the flesh, in order that the requirements of the Law might be fulfilled in us, who do not walk according to the flesh, but according to the Spirit" (Rom. 8:3-4). The person who depends on his own "flesh" for making heaven on earth is destined for disappointment. But the Scripture says, "Whoever believes in him shall not be disappointed" (Rom. 10:11).

Summing up, Spiritualism can in no sense be called Christianity. On all seven tests its stance is anti-Christian. Spiritualism does not accept the Bible as the final standard of faith and practice. It gives priority, not to the preaching of the gospel, but to spirit messages. It denies the deity of Christ, His substitutionary atonement and resurrection from the dead. No personal trust in the living Lord Jesus Christ is advocated and the hope of salvation rests not in divine grace but human attainment. Anyone who thinks that Spiritualism is Christian labors under a delusion — a delusion which may in fact be Satanically inspired. But God can deliver a soul from the grasp of Satan himself!

> The Lord's bond-servant must not be quarrelsome, but be kind to all, able to teach, patient when wronged, with gentleness correcting those who are in opposition, if perhaps God may grant them repentance leading to the knowledge of the truth, and they may come to their senses and escape from the snare of the devil, having been held captive by him to do his will (II Tim. 2:24-26).

A dramatic example of deliverance from demonic control was reported in *Christian Life,* January, 1952. In the inquiry room Evangelist W. Douglas Roe invited a girl of twelve and a middle-aged woman to accept Christ as their Savior from sin.

> Suddenly the young girl began to cry, "I can't accept Jesus Christ as my Savior! . . . I can't! . . . I can't! At this the older woman broke in, "I shouldn't have come here . . . I know I shouldn't."

She wrung her hands. "My spirit will be displeased . . . . I can't
see . . . There are balls of fire in front of my eyes!"

Then she explained she was a medium and that her spirit was
displeased with her presence at a gospel meeting. Rev. Roe under-
stood the problem, found out the name of the spirit, and asked God's
help. Then he took the woman by the wrist and said, "Red Blanket,
I charge you in the name of the Lord Jesus Christ, and through the
power of His shed blood, to leave this woman and this room now!"
At this the woman relaxed and said, "He is fading from my sight.
For the first time I can see you, Mr. Roe." During the next two days
while believers prayed he explained the gospel to her.

And on the closing night of the meetings, she was the first one to come
down the aisle as we sang "I've wandered far away from God, Lord,
I'm coming home." Her action seemed to release the power of the Holy
Spirit upon the meeting. Before we had finished singing, seventy-five
persons had come forward. And in that little church a real revival had
broken out as the powers of hell were overcome by the blood of the
Lord Jesus Christ.

Christians pray that other Spiritualists may be able to say with her,
"I know there is power in the name of Christ. For through his name
I have cast the spirits out of my home. And through His cleansing
blood, I now receive Him as my Savior and Lord."

FOOTNOTES

1. Palmer Emerson, "Can a Bad Individual Be at the Same Time a Good Spiritualist," *Centennial Book of Modern Spiritualism* (Chicago: The National Spiritualist Association of United States of America, 1948), p. 124.
2. Reginal Omez, *Psychical Phenomena*, translated by Renee Haynes, *Twentieth Century Encyclopedia of Catholicism*, Vol. 36 (New York: Hawthorne Books, 1958), p. 14.
3. Palmer Emerson, *op. cit.*, pp. 8-10.
4. *Time*, October 18, 1954, p. 62.
5. Robert P. Evans, "Normandy: Stronghold for Sorcerers," *Greater Europe Mission News Bulletin*, April, 1953, pp. 4-8.
6. Reginald Omez, *op. cit.*, p. 136.
7. Maurice Barbanell, *This Is Spiritualism* (London: Herbert Kenkins, 1959), p. 157.
8. *Ibid.*, p. 62.
9. *The National Spiritualist*, February, 1954, p. 2.
10. B. F. Austin, *The A. B. C. of Spiritualism* (Milwaukee: National Spiritualist Association Churches, n.d.), question 11.
11. T. Witton Davies, "Divination," *International Standard Bible Encyclopedia* II (Grand Rapids: Eerdmans Publishing Company, 1949), p. 861.
12. *The Endicott* (N.Y.) *Daily Bulletin*, April 4, 1957, p. 5.
13. See J. K. Van Baalen, *The Chaos of Cults* (Grand Rapids: Eerdmans Publishing Company, 1960, third revision), p. 43.
14. Oliver Lodge, *Raymond* (London: Methuen and Co., 1916), p. 194.
15. *The Binghamton* (N.Y.) *Press*, January 21, 1955, p. 8.
16. B. F. Austin, *op. cit.*, question 45.
17. G. W. Butterworth, *Spiritualism and Religion* (London: Society for Promoting Christian Knowledge, 1944), p. 142.
18. William James, *Memories and Studies* (New York: Longmans Green and Company, 1911), p. 174.
19. Eileen J. Garrett, *My Life: as a Search for the Meaning of Mediumship.* See G. W. Butterworth, *op. cit.*, pp. 161-62, 170-71, 182, and J. Stafford Wright, *Man in the Process of Time* (Grand Rapids: Wm. B. Eerdmans Publishing Company, 1956), p. 110.
20. Reginald Omez, *op. cit.*, pp. 30-33, 115-16.
21. Antony Flew, *A New Approach to Psychical Research* (London: Watts & Co., 1953), p. 136.
22. D. Mona Berry, "Comparisons," in *What Is Spiritualism?* ed. Emil C. Reichel (Milwaukee: National Spiritualist Association of Churches, n.d.), p. 39.
23. *Ibid.*, p. 38.
24. B. F. Austin, *op. cit.*, question 23.
25. G. W. Butterworth, *op. cit.*, pp. 101-102.
26. *Spiritualist Manual* (Milwaukee: NASC, 1955), p. 36.

27. George Lawton, *The Drama of Life After Death* (New York: Henry Holt & Co., 1932), p. 560.
28. *Ibid.*, p. 154.   29. *Ibid.*, p. 138.
30. *Spiritualist Manual*, p. 34.
31. *Ibid.*, pp. 35-36.
32. B. F. Austin, *op. cit.*, question 31.
33. *Ibid.*, question 65.   34. *Ibid.*, question 40.
35. *Ibid.*, questions 15, 16, 17.
36. Samuel Jacoby, in a mimeographed letter to Gordon R. Lewis, Pastor, People's Baptist Church, New Castle, Delaware, July 7, 1951.
37. George Lawton, *op. cit.*, p. 66.
38. *Ibid.*, p. 227.
39. *Centennial Book*, p. 24.
40. Frank D. Warren, "False Gods of Tradition," *The National Spiritualist*, April, 1954, p. 4.
41. B. F. Austin, *op. cit.*, question 19.
42. *Centennial Book*, p. 50.
43. Samuel Jacoby, *op. cit.*
44. Converse E. Nickerson, *Modern Spiritualism* (Milwaukee: National Spiritualist Association of Churches, 1959), p. 20.
45. Arthur Conan Doyle, *The New Revelation* (New York: George H. Doran Company, 1918), p. 55.
46. *Spiritualist Manual*, p. 69.
47. Meta H. Baker, "Teachers Department," *The National Spiritualist* Vol. 36, No. 357, April, 1954, p. 5.
48. B. F. Austin, *op. cit.*, question 83.
49. Maurice Barbanell, *op. cit.*, see photographs pp. 48, 88, 144, 176.
50. G. W. Butterworth, *op. cit.*, p. 92.
51. J. A. T. Robinson, "Resurrection in the N.T.," *The Interpreters Dictionary of the Bible IV* (New York: Abingdon Press, 1962), p. 47.
52. Robert J. MacDonald, "Faith and Works," in *What Is Spiritualism?* p. 34.
53. *Ibid.*
54. B. F. Austin, *op. cit.*, question 77.
55. Converse E. Nickerson, *op. cit.*, p. 34.
56. *Ibid.*
57. D. Mona Berry, *op. cit.*, p. 37.
58. *Spiritualist Manual*, p. 34.
59. Joseph P. Whitewell, *op. cit.*, pp. 35-36.
60. *Ibid.*, p. 76.
61. Thomas Grimshaw, *op. cit.*, p. 139.
62. Henry Wood, *op. cit.*, p. 143.
63. *Ibid.*, p. 145.   64. *Ibid.*, p. 148.   65. *Ibid.*, p. 189.
66. V. Douglas Roe. "I Clashed with the Spirit World," *Christian Life*, January, 1952, pp. 21, 64, 66.

FOR FURTHER STUDY

G. W. BUTTERWORTH, *Spiritualism and Religion* (London: Society for Promoting Christian Knowledge, 1944). A scholarly criticism of Spiritualism and its interpretations of Scripture in terms of Spiritualistic phenomena.

GEORGE LAWTON, *The Drama of Life After Death: A Study of Spiritualist Religion* (New York: Henry Holt and Company, 1932). A thorough description of Spiritualist beliefs and practices.

REGINALD OMEZ, *Psychical Phenomena, The Twentieth Century Encyclopedia of Catholicism* Vol. 36 (New York: Hawthorn Books, 1958). A survey of the history, subject matter and methods of psychical research with an evaluation by a Roman Catholic scholar.

J. STAFFORD WRIGHT, *Man in the Process of Time* (Grand Rapids: Wm. B. Eerdmans Publishing Company, 1956), p. 91-137. An evangelical's assessment of Spiritualism.

SUGGESTIONS FOR TEACHERS

Good teaching is marked by clarity of purpose. Review the content of this study and attempt to synthesize it in your own mind. This material may be divided into two sections for two teaching sessions. Put into a few words a statement of objectives for classroom presentation. *Confronting the Cults* differs from some other works on the subject in that its purpose is not primarily negative — refuting false doctrine, but positive — winning cultists to Christ.

1. Use the lead questions throughout the series to form the major divisions of the teaching sessions. Illustrate the way these questions keep discussion centered on the gospel by moving quickly back to them from irrelevant issues.

2. Anticipate replies Christians may expect to these questions from Spiritualists. Evaluate the Spiritualist position and give specific guidance in answering erroneous beliefs.

3. Build confidence for effective personal witness by helping your group to formulate possible approaches and answers. Use simple role playing situations to involve the group in learning the major doctrines of Spiritualism. After the material has been studied allow several people to take the position of the cultist in confronting the believer. Let others assume the role of a believer. Simulate a conversation. Try various ways of presenting truth in the face of error.

4. Ask members of the class to give their personal testimony of salvation by grace as they would to Spiritualists.

Spiritualists

SAMPLE LESSON PLAN

SESSION 1

Aim

To guide the class to a knowledge of Spiritualist teaching on religious authority and the gospel's importance.

To help the class develop skills of witnessing to those who accept spirit messages as a major source of religious truth.

Outline

A. Authority
   Question: "Do Spiritualists base their teachings on revelations other than the Bible?"

B. The Gospel's Priority
   Question: "Is the main business of Spiritualism the proclamation of the gospel? What is Spiritualism's major emphasis and what does the Bible say about it?"

Conclusion

Sum up the Spiritualist position and the best ways to help Spiritualists see The unique importance of the Bible and the gospel.

SESSION 2

Aim

To guide the class to a knowledge of Spiritualist teaching on the person of Christ, His death and resurrection and the need for personal trust in Christ and His grace alone.

Approach

Review briefly the previous lesson and set an attitude favorable to helping Spiritualists, not embarrassing them.

Outline

A. The Person of Christ
   Question: "Do Spiritualists believe that Jesus is the Christ, the eternal Word who became flesh?"

B. Redemption
   Question: "Do Spiritualists believe that Jesus died for their sins?"

C. The Resurrection of Jesus Christ
    Question: "Do Spiritualists believe that Jesus Christ arose from the dead?"

D. Personal Faith
    Question: "Do Spiritualists personally trust Jesus Christ as redeemer and Lord?"
    Question: "Do Spiritualists depend on some achievements of their own to provide justification or is it only by God's grace?"

Conclusion

Sum up the Scriptural teaching on these subjects and challenge the class to confront Spiritualists with the gospel.